CHESHIRE SHIPYARDS

by

Antony J Barratt

INTRODUCTION

When mention is made of shipbuilding in Cheshire the mind immediately springs to the name Cammell Laird, of Birkenhead, in the old county of Cheshire. Shipbuilding did however flourish elsewhere. Although neither the yards nor the craft built were as large or famous as those produced by Lairds, their place in history should nevertheless be recorded. The yards covered in this book are those which are or were sited in the post-1974 county of Cheshire.

On the River Dee shipbuilding took place at Chester (including Saltney just over the Welsh border), Neston and Parkgate. There were also other yards farther down the river, on the Welsh shore. On the Mersey building has taken place at Ellesmere Port, Runcorn, Widnes, Fiddlers Ferry, Sankey Bridges and Warrington, whilst yards also existed on the Weaver, at Frodsham, Northwich and Winsford.

Shipbuilding will have taken place elsewhere but not on a significant scale. In the era of wooden shipbuilding craft were often built in any convenient hollow adjacent to a river. Usually vessels were constructed for the builder's own use. Rarely did a site produce a flow of newly built craft, for other owners. Most ships were built, by "eye" with no, or the minimum of plans. With the move from wood to steel and sail to steam this was no longer an acceptable way of shipbuilding. Therefore if a yard was not able or prepared to adapt to the new building methods it eventually had no option but to go out of business.

In an effort to assist in securing an order some shipbuilders would take shares in a ship they built. This also helped to secure repeat orders and so ensure the continuation of the yard.

ABOUT THE AUTHOR

Antony Barratt was born in Northwich and attended Sir John Deane's Grammar School. The school was situated close to two of the yards covered in this book, namely the Pimblott and Yarwood yards. For several years on an almost daily basis he observed ships being built but little realised that he was watching the end of an era. This, together with a visit to Southampton in 1961, fired his interest in matters maritime. In the intervening years he has researched extensively the history of British shipping companies and locally-built ships. This research has resulted in the publication of over twenty articles on maritime history.

Published by Bernard McCall, 400 Nore Road, Portishead, Bristol, BS20 8EZ, England
(Telephone and fax : 01275 846178; e-mail : bmccall@globalnet.co.uk)
All distribution enquiries should be addressed to the publisher.
Printed by Dalton Printers, Dalton House, Thesiger Street, Cathays, Cardiff, CF2 4BN

ISBN : 1 902953-02-9

*Front cover : The former ICI barge **WINCHAM** was not too far from her birthplace in Northwich when she participated in the Mersey River Festival on 26 June 1982. She took part in a parade of ships in Birkenhead Docks on that date.*

*Back cover : The former Manchester Ship Canal tug **DARING** was even nearer to her Northwich birthplace when she was photographed on the Weaver Navigation at Acton Bridge on 23 July 1990.*

(Both photographs by Bernard McCall)

RIVER DEE

CHESTER

At Chester recorded shipbuilding commenced in 1680 when George Mainwaring built a ship on the Roodee, much to the annoyance of the authorities. Fifty years later there were two yards on the Roodee and in 1767 the River Dee Company established a yard there. This yard was to have five different occupiers commencing with Peter Jackson. He was succeeded in turn by William Courtney, William Mulvey, George Cramm and finally Messrs Cox & Miller, who vacated the site in 1869.

The second yard was occupied from 1783 by John & Joseph Troughton, then John Wilson & Sons, and finally by William Beshton until 1865. In 1795 it was claimed that craft up to 400 tons could be built on the Roodee. Vessels built significantly exceeded the 400 ton limit in later years. A dry dock was also built on the Ellesmere Canal in 1798. By the early 1800s, the industry at Chester was thriving. Up to twelve vessels could be in the process of building at any one time and about 250 men were employed in the yards.

The Roodee yards were located on the land until recently occupied by the gas holders, near Kitchen Street. When the newly constructed railway passed nearby, an unforeseen problem arose when a spark from a passing engine started a fire which caused considerable damage to the yard, then occupied by William Mulvey.

When ships were built of wood Chester was well situated with good sources of supply at Delamere and in North Wales. As a result shipbuilding at Chester exceeded that at Liverpool and continued to expand. William Courtney built several warships for the Royal Navy including the 24-gun **EDEN**, which managed to lose two whole crews, to fever, whilst on anti slavery patrols off West Africa. During the American War of Independence the Chester-built, 26-gun, **LEVANT** was captured by the American frigate **CONSTITUTION**, after a four hour battle on 20 February 1815. She was eventually recaptured by the Royal Navy off the Azores a short time later. Her adversary, the **CONSTITUTION**, is now preserved at Boston, USA, whilst she herself was broken up around 1820.

Mulvey built the small sailing ship **ANN MULVEY** in 1842. Like many ships at the time she was owned in 64th portions, ownership being divided between thirteen individuals including other members of the Mulvey family. After twenty years service the vessel was sold to Amlwch owners. Eventually she was lost in the Bristol Channel in April 1887.

Earlier, in 1827, Mulvey had built the steam cargo vessel **HERALD**, for the Liverpool Steam Navigation Company. Eight years later she was purchased by the St George Company (owners of the **SIRIUS**, the first steamer to cross the Atlantic in 1838). The **HERALD** salvaged the brig **ALEXANDER ROBERTSON** in 1838. The fate of the **HERALD** is not known but it is thought she was broken up prior to 1843.

Early ships built at Chester worked in many parts of the world. Courtney built East and West Indiamen, whilst steamers were built for use at Philadelphia and New York. Later ships were built for service in West Africa and Australia.

M. Corne, p.

Levant

A. Anderson, sc.

Cyane

THE CONSTITUTION TAKING THE CYANE AND LEVANT,

Constitution

(34)   (21)

off Madeira   28 Feby 1815

*On the previous page, reference was made to **LEVANT**. In this print, the American frigate **CONSTITUTION** is seen with **CYANE** and **LEVANT** off Madeira. **LEVANT** is the smaller vessel to the left of centre. The work is attributed to Michaele Felice (as artist) and Anderson, Alexander (as engraver).*

(Courtesy National Maritime Museum, London)

Built at Chester as **RUBY**, the **MOSSDALE** was purchased by the Shropshire Union Canal Company in 1867 for £350 and used in the canal company's carrying fleet. The Canal Company withdrew from the carrying trade in 1921 when the **RUBY** was sold to Richard Abel & Company. Renamed **MOSSDALE** she was used to carry grain, often on the Bridgewater Canal. Rebuilt in 1933 at Abel's yard at Runcorn she continued in service until the mid-1960s when Richard Abel & Company were taken over by Hoveringham Gravel. The new owners wished to concentrate on the aggregates trade and ceased lighterage operations. The **MOSSDALE** was disposed of for possible conversion to a restaurant. Laid up at Northwich, the conversion never materialised and in 1971 the craft was donated to the fledgling Ellesmere Port Boat Museum. Since arriving at the Museum the **MOSSDALE** has been substantially rebuilt.

(Author)

In 1856 Messrs Cox & Miller took over the River Dee Company yard from George Cramm who had been forced out of business as a result of the losses he had incurred on building the 2719 ton **ROYAL CHARTER** at Queensferry in 1854. After five years of service carrying emigrants to Australia in partnership with the **GREAT BRITAIN** (now preserved at Bristol), the **ROYAL CHARTER** was blown ashore on Anglesey in October 1859 with the loss of 459 lives. The storm was one of the most savage ever experienced and caused the loss of over 130 other ships, badly damaging a further 90, and led to a total death toll of over 800. However the greatest single loss was the **ROYAL CHARTER**, after which the gale was named.

During their occupation of the River Dee Company's yard, Messrs Cox & Miller built a series of large iron sailing ships. These included the **GITANA**, 1366 tons, which had the distinction of being wrecked twice. The first occasion was off Denmark in 1883. Salvaged, she was eventually lost of Cape Horn in 1897 whilst the **CHESHIRE,** 1233 tons, went missing on her maiden voyage to Calcutta in 1865.

At the end of the nineteenth century a small yard operated by William Roberts was located close to Chester Castle. This yard concentrated on building small working and pleasure craft. It moved to the canal basin around 1906. In 1914, J H and W S Taylor was formed and opened a repair yard in the Dee Basin. Six years later, Taylors rented the graving dock along with premises adjacent to the North Basin. Boats were built here. In 1926, part of the former Shropshire Union Canal Company yard was occupied with the rest of the yard coming under Taylor control in 1936. As the use of commercial wooden craft declined, Taylor built a number of cabin cruisers. Boat repairing still continues at this site along with the occasional building of wooden craft, including in recent years some for museums. In the mid-1990s, the future of the yard looked bleak. However, at the time of publication, there is a possibility that part of the yard may survive as a centre for training people in the art of wooden boat building.

For many years the Shropshire Union Canal Company built and repaired barges at Chester and Ellesmere Port. Amongst the barges built in the 1880s were twenty-two for which the sections had been built at Crewe Locomotive Works.

As the estuary silted up anchorages were opened up, down river, nearer the sea and shipbuilding followed.

*The **AMARYLLIS** is one of a number of cabin cruisers built at the Taylor yard in Chester. This 30 ft cabin cruiser was built as the **TEAL** and she can often be seen at the Ellesmere Port Boat Museum.*

(Author)

*In December 1998, several barges were being excavated in the North Basin at Tower Wharf, Chester. They had been buried for forty years and had to be removed as the basin was being excavated for a marina. Sections of three of the ten found were lifted in December 1999 and taken to Ellesmere Port Boat Museum for preservation. From various press reports, it appears that the vessel at the top of the picture, **HERBERT**, is one of these. Of the others, **JOHN** is at the very bottom of the picture with just an angle iron showing. The third vessel, **ONWARD**, is not in the picture. Other locations where discarded vessels were buried include the Dee Basin, Chester (33 vessels); West Bank Dock and Spike Island, Widnes; and Bridgewater Locks, Big and Little Pools, Runcorn. Vessels were also scuttled at the entrance to Winsford Flashes and at Sutton Weaver near Frodsham. Some are still visible at the latter location.* *(Author)*

PARKGATE & NESTON

At Neston and Parkgate several small shipbuilders quickly came and went. The most productive was the partnership of Thomas Makin and John Washington, which lasted for five years from 1785. In that time they produced eleven ships, including three for the Parkgate Packet Company in which John Washington held an interest. This dynamic partnership ended when John Washington died, forcing Thomas Makin into bankruptcy. The Parkgate Packet Company traded principally between Parkgate and Ireland with such locally-built vessels as the **KING** (1785) and **QUEEN** (1786), both of 100 grt, and **PRINCESS ROYAL** (1787), of 134 grt.

SALTNEY

Although Saltney is just in Wales, it is appropriate to consider it in any survey of Cheshire shipbuilding. J Crichton & Company, which had opened a yard at Connah's Quay in 1910, opened a second yard in 1913 at Saltney. Over the next 22 years, the company constructed a multiplicity of vessels, including tugs, tankers, cargo ships, paddle steamers and harbour craft, for use at both at home and overseas. Building ceased in 1935 when the yard was purchased by National Shipbuilders Security Limited. This organisation had been set up by the shipbuilding industry to buy and close shipyards and so help the remaining yards weather the depression of the 1930s. Once a yard had been purchased a covenant was placed on the land preventing its use for shipbuilding, for at least 40 years. This restriction therefore marked the end of major shipbuilding at Saltney and Chester.

This view of the Crichton yard from the opposite bank of the River Dee is believed to date from the early 1920s. Several craft are under construction. The fitting out wharf is at the far left of the photograph.

(Flintshire Record Office)

The **ST CYRUS** was built at the Crichton yard at Saltney in 1919. On 12 December 1930 whilst towing the sloop **HMS SNAPDRAGON** from Portland to Gibraltar with her Crichton-built sistership **ST GENNY**, she was struck by a heavy wave and badly damaged. The **ST GENNY** was also struck by the wave but was less fortunate and sank, 5 of her crew of 28 being picked up by the crippled **ST CYRUS**. After repairs, **ST CYRUS** was engaged in towing targets for gunnery practice. She was lost on 22 January 1941 after striking a mine off the Humber.

Between **ST CYRUS** and the Crichton wharf can be seen another sistership, **ST FLORENCE**, being fitted out. The **ST FLORENCE** was purchased by the Canadian Pacific Railway Company in 1924. Renamed **KYUQUOT**, she served at Vancouver until broken up in 1962. The wharf in the background of the above photograph is the Saltney Wharf of the Great Western Railway Company.

(Flintshire Record Office)

The **COBURG** of the Alexandra Towing Company was a near-sister to the same company's **SALTHOUSE** which was the last vessel built at the Saltney yard. The **COBURG** served at Liverpool, as well as for the Admiralty at Devonport between 25 August 1939 and 14 October 1940, remaining on war service until 1941. She was finally broken up at Preston in 1965. A similar fate befell the **SALTHOUSE**.   (Flintshire Record Office)

The **INDE** was completed by Crichton in 1924 for the Nigerian Transport Company. She was typical of many craft built by small British shipbuilders for service on rivers throughout the Empire. The decline of this market was one of the factors in the closure of a number of smaller yards. She was 105 feet long and had a speed of ten knots. She remained in service until the late 1950s and was eventually broken up in West Africa.

                                   (Flintshire Record Office)

*Typical of many earlier coasters the **RADSTOCK** was built by Crichton in 1925. Of 195 grt and 105 feet long, she is seen alongside the fitting-out wharf. She was built for the Somerset & Dorset Railway Company to carry locomotive coal from South Wales to Highbridge. Sold in 1934 to Captain Morse, Watchet, she was used in the late 1930s and in the early part of the Second World War on charter to the RAF to recover radio controlled aeroplanes ("Queen Bees") from the sea off Doniford, Somerset. Requisitioned as a store ship in 1940, she spent much of the war in Portsmouth. After service with Bristowe Shippers Ltd, Bristol, she was broken up in 1958.*

(Flintshire Record Office)

*The Norwegian heavy lift ship **BELRAY** is seen at Birkenhead loaded with a dozen barges built by Crichton. This method of ship delivery was often used to fulfil overseas orders.*

(Flintshire Record Office)

*In the 1920s, Crichton built several grain elevators for service at Liverpool. In this view, **PNEUMATIC ELEVATOR No 6**, built in 1924, is at work in the dock system. She was listed as still being in use in 1975. This type of craft, which sucked grain from the holds of ships and transferred it to barges, was eventually rendered redundant on Merseyside by the concentration of the grain trade into Liverpool's Royal Seaforth Dock.*

(Flintshire Record Office)

RIVER MERSEY

ELLESMERE PORT

Before the opening of the Ellesmere Canal in 1795, the town now known as Ellesmere Port did not exist. However the canal company decided to build extensive warehousing plus slipways to maintain the many barges operating on the canal and across the Mersey. As early as 1810, land was being leased to a Ralph Manley to use for barge building. This lease was soon taken over by Thomas Telford, whether for himself or the Canal Company is not clear. Another plot of land was leased in 1817 by John Grace specifically to build two vessels. Land on the foreshore was taken over for shipbuilding by a Mr Haselden in 1825. How successful this venture was is not clear, for in 1828 the yard, its contents and a partly built flat were advertised for sale. This yard eventually came under the control of the Shropshire Union Canal Company, which extended it and enhanced the facilities for its own use. Further changes were made in the 1850s Including the provision of a Patent Slip for hauling craft out of the water for repair. This Slip had a number of lessees including Mason & Co, who withdrew from the lease very quickly, and, from 1863, a Mr Peake. The site of part of this slipway is still visible. Dry docks were also provided at Ellesmere Port for both narrow boats and larger canal craft.

Following the construction of the Manchester Ship Canal, a group of Tyneside shipbuilders and repairers set up repair yards at Manchester and at Ellesmere Port. The Ellesmere Port repair yard which covered about seven acres was opened in October 1893 and built four coasters during the 1920s. The first pair were ordered by the wartime Shipping Controller, whilst the second pair appear to have been laid down as a speculative venture. The fourth vessel, **PENSTONE**, was laid down in 1919 and was substantially complete in 1921 but not launched until June 1925 or completed until August 1926. The period taken to build these vessels may indicate that construction was undertaken to keep the workforce of usefully employed when routine repair work was in short supply, or completion was deferred because of the depressed trading conditions of the times.

The first of the four coasters, built by the Manchester Dry Dock Company Ltd (as the company was known after 1906) was named **BEN SEYR** and owned by the Ramsey Steamship Company Ltd of the Isle of Man. Presumably the company was satisfied with the vessel as it acquired on the second hand market two more of the group. The **BEN SEYR** was lost without trace whilst on a voyage from Ramsey to Cardiff in October 1938. The two purchased by the company remained in service until broken up, one in 1957, **BEN VARREY**, and the other, **BEN AIN**, in 1963. By this time the **BEN AIN** was the last single hatch steam coaster serving on the Irish Sea. The fourth vessel had been sunk in a collision in Liverpool Bay in July 1948. The Ellesmere Port yard closed in 1969 at which time 150 workers lost their jobs.

RUNCORN

Farther up the estuary at Runcorn shipbuilding thrived between 1778 and 1886, when the construction of larger ships was made impracticable due to the building of the Ship Canal. However barge building continued until the construction of the **RUTH BATE** at Abel's yard, in 1953. Steamers were launched at Runcorn as early as 1816 when the **PRINCE REGENT** and the **DUKE OF WELLINGTON** were built for a Liverpool, Runcorn and Warrington passenger service.

Before the Ship Canal was built, the size of vessel the yards at Runcorn could build was restricted only by the depth of channel into which hulls could be launched. The channels in the Mersey are notorious for moving, even from one side of the river to the other. For most of the shipbuilding period the channels which at that time skirted the Runcorn shore did not favour the construction of the largest ships. Nevertheless Runcorn benefited as the smaller shipbuilders of Liverpool were forced out of business by high rents or the expansion of the Liverpool dock system. The yards were sited along what is now Mersey Road.

The first recorded launching was the brig **COOPER** in 1778, by an unknown builder. Wm Wright with various partners appears from 1802 as a shipbuilder. In 1816 Wright's daughter married Dennis Brundrit, a druggist and owner of Stenhills Quarry, at Runcorn. In 1823 Brundrit joined a partnership with Philip Whiteway. It was this undertaking which went onto become the main Runcorn yard and to build the most notable ships constructed in the town. Before looking at these ships it is appropriate to mention some of the other local builders.

The Old Quay Yard, founded by the Mersey & Irwell Navigation Company, built barges from about 1837 mainly for company use. The Castle Rock Yard was situated where the road bridge now stands and was occupied by John Anderton. Taken over by Philip Speakman in 1869, the yard eventually passed to Richard Abel & Sons who continued to operate the yard until it closed in the early 1960s. Anderton built a number of schooners at the yard for his own use.

To the east of the Castle Rock Yard was the Belvedere Yard. This yard was also in use by 1840 and built not only flats but also a number of seagoing craft. The yard closed in 1879. Brundrit's Yard came next and then the Old Quay Yard. Other builders at Runcorn included W Evans, Okell & Webster, Wm Rigby, J Rawlinson, John Weedall and T & J Johnson. However the records of the work of these builders are very limited.

The Castle Rock Yard survived as a barge repair and building yard whilst the former Brundrit slipway became a public slipway for general repairs. The other part of the Brundrit Yard was leased out as a repair yard and continued in use until the 1930s.

The Castle Rock yard is beneath the arches at the left hand side of the above photograph which shows the Runcorn foreshore in 1892/93 during the building of the Manchester Ship Canal. The remains of other slipways are visible in the foreground. The author's photograph on the right shows how little remains of the yard in 1997.

Mention has already been made of the paddle steamers built in 1816. A further eight steamers were built by the local yards which also launched over 160 sailing craft and innumerable barges during their existence. Notable among the sailing craft were:-

The **JANE**, built as a sloop in 1800 and re-rigged as a ketch in 1881. After trading locally until 1847 she was sold to owners on Anglesey and is thought to have been sold to Bristol Channel owners twelve years later. She was hulked in 1925 and used as a coal store. In 1936, she sank at her mooring at Lydney. At this time she was reputed to be the oldest British-registered merchant vessel still in existence.

The **SNOWFLAKE** may even be still afloat. This two-masted schooner built by Brundrit in 1880 was engaged in the Newfoundland salt fish trade until the start of the First World War. Initially owned locally by J Foulkes & Co, Runcorn, she was later used to carry china clay from Cornwall to Runcorn for onward carriage to the Potteries. In 1934, she was sold to Yugoslav owners who fitted her with an engine and renamed her **HRVAT**. Thus named she left Plymouth in 1935 with a cargo of clay for the Mediterranean. She was disabled on passage and was towed into Santander. She was trading out of Marseilles in 1938. During the German occupation of Yugoslavia, the **HRVAT** is reputed to have served with the Partisans. Taken over by the Yugoslav Government in 1949, she was still in use in 1975. If she has survived the traumatic convulsions which have beset that country, the vessel will be 120 years old. Survival could just be possible as she underwent major reconstruction in 1949 and 1960. There are rumours that she was being used for tourist trips in the 1980s.

It was quite common for the owners of sailing ships to commission paintings of their ships. This painting of the **SNOWFLAKE** *is reproduced by kind permission of Mr Wm Leathwood, of Runcorn.*

Four years after his death the Brundrit family launched, for their own use, the largest vessel built in any of the local yards. The appropriately named, three-masted ship, **DENNIS BRUNDRIT** was launched in 1856 and measured 462 tons. Even though not large by the standards of the day she traded world wide. On rounding Cape Horn in 1879 for the twentieth time, she was badly damaged but was able to make the Falkland Islands. Sold there for use as a coal hulk she resumed trading again in 1884. This time she made nine voyages to London before being wrecked once more in the Falklands.

In 1894 the Manchester Ship Canal Company, which had also purchased the Bridgewater Canal, transferred barge repairs from the Old Quay Yard to a newly built yard known locally as the Sprinch Yard. The yard was built in an abandoned loop of the Bridgewater Canal. Officially called the Victoria Dockyard, it must have been one of the finest installations in the country. Provided were boiler, fitting, blacksmith's and wheelwright shops plus a sawmill. Four dry docks could accommodate up to six barges simultaneously. At the yard however only three barges were built. These were the **CORONATION**, **EMPIRE** and **CARRIER**, built between 1911 and 1913.

The Sprinch yard closed in 1977, to make way for new roads. Buried at the yard and in the adjoining Big Pool are numerous old barges. This was the end for many of these fine craft. Others lie buried along the line of the old Bridgewater locks, at Runcorn, in the old West Bank Dock and Spike Island at Widnes.

*When built in 1953, the **RUTH BATE** was the last cargo-carrying vessel constructed at Runcorn and the last wooden barge built on any of the three rivers. After use in the carrying trades, for several years she was used as the HQ for the Maghull Branch of the St Johns Ambulance Brigade. The barge was eventually sold to an enthusiast for restoration, which was not carried out. She was purchased by Halton Borough Council with the long term aim of restoration. Towed to Widnes 1988, she lay submerged in the St Helen's Canal, and was broken up at Widnes in May 1999, as seen in the photograph on the right.*

(Author)

WIDNES

Widnes was a shipbuilding centre on a small scale between 1861 and 1890. Shipbuilding at Widnes seems to have coincided with a shift in the river channels, making shipbuilding at Runcorn more difficult. During these years nine craft are known to have been built, being five schooners, three flats and a wooden-hulled steamer. The latter was the 74-ton **HETTIE**, built in 1879 and remaining intact until 1949.

Two slipways appear on maps, one near St Mary's Road was probably the site occupied by Wm Cooper, who operated a large fleet of barges and dredgers into the 1960s. The other was just to the east of the Widnes wet dock on the piece of land known as Spike Island, where the St Helens Canal enters the Mersey. With the demise of shipbuilding at the Spike Island yard, it was taken over and upgraded by Wm Cooper for repair work.

WARRINGTON

For a short period the river channels and other factors favoured iron shipbuilding at Warrington. The existence of good rail communications to bring Lancashire coal and Staffordshire iron helped shipbuilding to flourish. Wooden shipbuilding had been undertaken in the eighteenth century, mainly for local traders and routes. Warrington's halcyon years were from 1840 to 1857. During this period at least 20 iron vessels were built.

The yard responsible for building these vessels was at Bank Quay which was associated with the Bank Quay Foundry Company. The yard was leased to various operators including, Tayleur Sanderson & Company, Tayleur & Company and eventually came under the control of the Bank Quay Foundry Company in 1856. The yard was extended in 1847 to permit the building of larger vessels. However, in 1857, with yet another change in the river channels, the ending of the Crimean War and the availability of better sites in other parts of England, shipbuilding at Warrington came to an abrupt end. The Bank Quay yard was advertised for sale, but finding no buyers the yard and its contents were sold off separately in 1860.

*Completed in 1853 at a cost of £34,000 the **TAYLEUR** was built at the Bank Quay Foundry yard. When launched she was claimed to be the largest sailing ship built in England. Fully rigged her tonnage was 1997 tons and she was able to carry 4,000 tons of cargo. Owned by Charles A Moore & Company and chartered to Pilkington & Wilson, the founders of the original White Star Line, she left Liverpool, on her maiden voyage, on Thursday, 19 January 1854, destined for Australia. Aboard were 652 people, including the crew. Soon after departure she encountered rough weather. On the Saturday morning she found herself close to the Irish coast, with the wind forcing her ever closer to land. Despite having dropped both anchors the force of wind and sea caused the anchor chains to snap allowing her to drift onto rocks. Unable to launch lifeboats one passenger swam to the shore with a rope. However the vessel was washed out to sea and with it 380 lives were lost.*

(Warrington Museum)

Bank Quay was not the only location where ships were built in the Warrington area. Messrs Clare & Ridgway had a yard at Sankey Bridges for 122 years. Founded in 1807, by William Clare, the yard repaired the craft used in his coal carrying business. He was later joined by John Clare and they went on to build over 20 vessels for their own account. After 1846 craft were also built for other local shipowners. The exact date when the yard became Clare & Ridgway is not known but it was trading as such in 1867. Shipbuilding continued until 1913 while ship repairing continued until 1929. In all Clare & Ridgway built around 40 vessels.

*Built in 1906 by Clare & Ridgway, the **SANTA ROSA** was an example of a type of vessel known as a jigger flat. That meant that she had two masts instead of the more usual single mast. She was the last vessel of the type to be built when she was launched for the United Alkali Company and was designed to carry limestone to the company's plants at Widnes and Fleetwood. Following the merger of United Alkali and ICI, the use of unpowered flats on coastal voyages ceased. After being sold, she was fitted with an auxiliary motor and continued to trade until destroyed by fire when at anchor in the River Dee off Llanerch-y-mor in 1934. Her sistership, the **EUSTACE CAREY**, was used as a barge until 1965 when she was beached at Spike Island, Widnes, where her hull was later burnt to the waterline. Her rudder has been preserved nearby.*

(Warrington Museum)

Other lesser shipbuilders at Sankey Bridges built about fifty other craft. Shipbuilding also took place at nearby Fiddlers Ferry. The sixteen flats built by a T Wilkinson and a W Wilkinson were launched into the Mersey between 1859 and 1885. A further three flats were launched into the Sankey Navigation by Messrs Hill and Grundy between 1877 and 1880. Towards the end of the Great War a number of concrete coasters and barges were built at Fiddlers Ferry by Concrete Seacraft Limited. The largest vessels of the series being the **CRETECAMP** of 1919 and the **CRETECOVE** of 1920. Both were vessels of about 710 grt.

RIVER WEAVER

Perhaps surprisingly the most prolific area for shipbuilding in the county was the mid-Cheshire stretch of the River Weaver. Although many miles from the sea, over 2000 craft were built at Northwich and Winsford in the 250 years to 1971. The Weaver was made navigable by virtue of an Act of Parliament passed in 1721, on the sixth attempt. Canalisation was needed to allow the salt trade to prosper.

NORTHWICH

Shipbuilding at Northwich commenced in the 1730s. The early craft were not large, as the river at that time could only accommodate vessels with a draught of 4.5ft. These craft had a cargo capacity of up to 40 tons if working to Northwich and 28 tons, if going to Winsford. The size of the vessels built was governed by the dimensions of the river and its locks. Fortunately for much of its existence the Weaver Navigation Trustees pursued a dynamic policy of improvement and enlargement.

Early information about shipbuilding on the river is sparse. Trade Directories show a fluctuating number of shipbuilders at Northwich over the years:-

1822/3	3	1860	7
1828/9	2	1874	4
1834	1	1878	6
1850	4	1890	4
1857	1	1906	2

Many builders lasted but a short time, as entry into the trade required little capital. However, the ups and downs of trade cycles caused many to quit the business almost as quickly as they entered it. Over the decade 1850 to 1860 for instance, the number of shipbuilders recorded at Northwich went from 4 to 1 to 7.

The end of that decade saw a rationalisation of the salt industry which led to an increase in orders for new craft. More significantly iron hulls began to be built. The hull plating for some of the first iron ships coming from redundant salt pans. These powered craft became known as "Weaver packets".

Prominent amongst the builders who did not survive into the twentieth century were the Okell and the Gibson families. Different members of the Okell family occupied a site, immediately north of where the Hayhurst Bridge now stands for over 80 years. The Gibson family operated the Witton Dockyard for about 60 years. This yard was sited just north of Barons Quay, not far from the present Marks & Spencer store.

With the consolidation of the industry two shipbuilders came to dominate the scene, namely W J Yarwood & Sons and Isaac Pimblott & Sons.

The building of ships on the Yarwood site, off Navigation Road, can be traced back to at least 1840. It was then that John Thompson, of Macclesfield, commenced building wooden vessels, some steam powered, in an abandoned meander of the river. He was succeeded in 1885 by John Woodcock who had been apprenticed to Thompson as a carpenter. Woodcock's ownership was to be relatively short for he died in September 1896, aged 56 years. Yarwood purchased the yard a month after the death of John Woodcock. This ensured the continued employment for the 40 men and the completion of the craft on the stocks at the time, one of which, *HIBERNIA*, was the first steel-hulled vessel for Brunner Mond & Company Ltd.

William Yarwood had been born in 1851 and was the son of a Northwich shoemaker. After an apprenticeship as a blacksmith he went to work for the Weaver Navigation Trustees.

On taking over the yard in October 1896, Yarwood started to develop the facilities so that as much of each vessel as possible could be constructed by the company. As well as developing the Woodcock site the company acquired further land to permit expansion, which included the building of steam engines, for both marine and other uses. Over the next sixty years more than 200 steam engines were built. A foundry, machine shop and design office were provided. Work was also undertaken for other local non-shipping industries.

Gradually iron and then steel replaced wood as the preferred hull material. The last major wooden Weaver packet but not the last wooden vessel built, was launched in 1907. Four years later the diesel-powered packet **EGBERT** was built and as such must have been one of the earliest motor vessels built in Britain.

After the 1914-18 war the company began to produce a more varied mix of vessels. By 1926 the yard had expanded to employ about 250 men. Twenty years later this had increased to 300 men and the yard covered 8 acres, had 9 building berths plus a repair berth and could build ships up to 160 feet long.

As well as building vessels for the Admiralty, craft were also built, perhaps surprisingly, for the Royal Air Force. The largest of these was the **RAFA AQUARIUS**, which was designed for use at Singapore.

This 113 foot long vessel was variously described as a "flying boat stores ship", "refuelling vessel", "recovery ship" and "water carrier". Whatever her role the vessel appeared to be fitted with a sophisticated array of radio aerials. Such characteristics may lend support to the unsubstantiated claim that she was to be used as a radio relay or monitoring ship, designed to monitor Japanese military radio traffic in war torn China. This possibility may also be supported by the fact that during construction the craft was supervised by Aircraftsman T. E. Shaw. Aircraftsman Shaw was better known as Lawrence of Arabia. He had re-enlisted in the RAF as a radio and marine specialist after leaving the Army. She was sunk on 14 February 1942 near Tjibea Island, north of Banka, off the south-east coast of Sumatra with the loss of 60 - 70 lives.

The **AQUARIUS** was an oil-fired steamer, her compound engine developing 330 ihp. Her dimensions were 113' x 22' 6" x 10' 6". She sailed under her own steam to Singapore, averaging a speed of eight knots for the voyage.

(Cheshire Record Office)

The four photographs on this page are reproduced from a Yarwood brochure. This aerial view may date from 1937/38. The third vessel from the bridge in the upper left could be the dredger **MORMUGAO** being built for India. If so, the tugs are possibly the Admiralty sisters **TRUNNION** and **TAMPEON**. The three large white hulls are possibly dumb barges built for John Holt & Co Ltd, of Liverpool.

This view of work underway in the plate shop is sadly undated but it could possibly be a late 1940s view.

This is a picture of the 'slab' where the frames were bent, with bending taking place.

The brochure says that these passenger barges (yard numbers 607 and 608), destined for Sudan, were 110' x 21' x 5' 6". They were constructed then dismantled for shipment and subsequent re-erection. Built in 1938 for service on the Nile, they were based in Khartoum. About this time, Yarwoods also built three other barges for the Sudan government. Yard number 606 was a "twin screw motor ferry". Yard numbers 693 and 694 were 90 ft barges.

Seen in knock-down form and boxed ready for shipment, this vessel is described by the brochure as a "shallow draft river steamer", one of five built and engined for John Holt & Co (Liverpool) Ltd for service in West Africa.

(All photographs courtesy of Cheshire Record Office)

Merchant vessels were built in great numbers at the Yarwood yard. Many enjoyed great longevity but some came to unfortunate ends, occasionally after only a short time in service.

The tanker **BP EXPLORER**, built by Yarwood in 1957 capsized in January 1961 off Avonmouth. The upturned hull was swept twenty miles up river. All five crew were lost. Having been salvaged and renamed, she met problems in the Bristol Channel a second time, twelve months later. On this occasion she ran aground at Nash Point on the Glamorgan coast but the crew were thankfully saved. The tanker herself was declared a constructive total loss.

In the early 1960s Yarwood built a class of three lighterage tugs for the Rea Company of Liverpool. The **ELMGARTH**, having been renamed **BARKIS**, was lost off Lowestoft in 1976 whilst assisting a tanker. Three of the crew were saved but one man was lost. The wreck was eventually blown up. Ten years after the loss of the **BARKIS**, her sister the **PINEGARTH**, was also lost off Lowestoft but with no casualties. At the time she was named **ALA**.

The third ship of the class, the **CHERRYGARTH**, also capsized but was salvaged and sold to Greece in 1990. She was renamed **MADONNA** and was eventually scrapped in 1995. These tugs, having been built for lighterage work, were unsuited to towage in open seas.

Another tug which was lost was the **SEA VOLUNTEER** built by Yarwood in 1963 to work at Bristol. Twenty years later, she was sold to Panamanian flag operators and renamed **WRESTLER**. Sold again in 1987 she was converted into a fishing vessel. Her career in this new role was short for later in 1987, she was lost in an Atlantic storm under the **IMMANUEL II**.

A Yarwood-built tug became the centre of a diplomatic incident in 1942. The **NUNEATON** was built in 1935 and shipped out to West Africa. This 42 ton vessel was one of two tugs used by the Special Operations Executive in "Operation Postmaster", a clandestine raid on the Spanish harbour of Fernando Po. The larger tug took in tow an interned Italian liner whilst the **NUNEATON** extracted the German vessel **LIKOMBA** and the powered lighter **BIBUNDI**. A considerable diplomatic row blew up over the attack on a neutral port. It is known that the tug was still afloat in 1985 though no further details are available.

A number of vessels were built, for Lever Brothers. These included the **SAND SWALLOW II**, built by Yarwood in 1947 and designed to replace an earlier Yarwood-built dredger, the **SAND SWALLOW** of 1923. The purpose of both vessels was to maintain the depth of water at the Bromborough Pool and Dock complex. Although sold by Lever Brothers, the 1947-built ship is still in existence but her days are numbered for she lies at a breaker's yard at New Holland on the Humber at the time of writing.

*The **SAND SWALLOW II** lies on the slipway of the breaker's yard at New Holland on the south bank of the Humber in April 1996.*

(Roy Cressey)

The tales of Para Handy immortalized the tiny Scottish Puffer. These small vessels were the delivery vans of the Western Isles. All sorts of cargoes were carried which were often off loaded whilst the craft lay high and dry on an island beach. In the 1950s Yarwood built two of the more modern examples of such vessels although both were surprisingly steam propelled.

The **MOONLIGHT**, of 1952, could carry about 170 tons of cargo. The **STORMLIGHT** built five years later could well have been the last of the thousands of steamships built in Britain. She was certainly the last steam coaster.

*Looking her best in bright sunlight, the **STORMLIGHT** is a fine example of a Yarwood-built coaster.*

(Cheshire Museum Service)

*The largest ship built on the Weaver was the tanker **ATHELBRAE**, built in 1955 by Yarwood for their parent company's use in British Guiana, the vessel measured 668 tons. She was broken up in 1979.*

(Cheshire Museum Service)

Yarwood had built many narrow boats and it fell to them, jointly with Pimblott, to build the Admiral class of barges, which were the last major group of canal barges to be built in Britain at the beginning of the 1960s. The order was divided between Pimblott (8 craft) and Yarwood (4 craft).

*The **KEPPEL** is one of the last barges to have been built in Britain. She was photographed, with sister vessel **LINDSAY** moored inside her, on the Trent and Mersey Canal by the Anderton Boat Lift. The barges were built in 1961 and 1960 respectively. All named after admirals, they were designed to offer maximum carrying capacity. The bows of the barges were different - the Pimblott-built boats had a semi-circular bow whilst those built by Yarwood had a slightly more traditional bow which improved handling.*

(Author)

In 1946 the Yarwood yard was sold to the United Molasses Group and was run as a subsidiary of the Athel Line Ltd. During the 1950s, output shifted from barges, dredgers and local craft and became concentrated on tug building for both home and overseas markets.

In the 1960s the United Molasses Group decided to divest itself of a number of subsidiaries, one being the Northwich shipyard. Due to the limited space for expansion and the limitation on the size of vessels which could be built, the decision was taken to concentrate work in another yard the Group owned at Lowestoft. The Northwich yard closed following the delivery of the tug **ST ELMO** in November 1965. This brought to an end of 125 years of shipbuilding on the site.

*A fine view of the **ST ELMO** on trials in the River Mersey.*   *(Cheshire Museum Service)*

The other major Northwich shipyard was that of Isaac Pimblott & Sons whose family started shipbuilding in the mid-nineteenth century. The original site was near to Hayhurst Bridge. However, due to the restricted nature of this location the yard was moved, in 1906, to a new site, upstream of Hunts Locks. This allowed a yard to be laid out free of the constraints of having to accommodate existing installations. From 1912 the old yard was occupied as a repair yard by the Liverpool Lighterage Company and remained in use until 1972.

Success accompanied the move and the yard was expanded in 1918 and further modernised during the Second World War. The ongoing investment allowed the Company, like Yarwood, to expand into supplying the wider UK market as well as overseas customers. Continued success is reflected in the Pimblott Company's records with the entry in 1954 that bonuses totalling £900 be paid to the directors, £100 to the "upstairs" staff and £75 to the "downstairs" staff.

Britain's withdrawal from empire led to a contraction in the overseas markets for both companies. This contraction was accompanied by a reduction in local orders leading to a decline in the trading outlook. The Yarwood yard closed and a similar option was considered by the Pimblott family. However, orders from the Admiralty for several fleet tenders and tugs staved off the fateful day. During this respite a number of possibilities were considered including developing the yard as a marina. In 1971 the decision was taken to cease trading and the yard subsequently did become a marina. The Yarwood yard has not been so fortunate. Most of the site is now covered by housing and light industry.

Both Yarwood and Pimblott repaired vessels as well as building them. Between 1902 and 1938, Yarwood's records show that on average nearly sixty vessels a year underwent repairs. This must have been particularly useful in the depressed 1930s, when the average rose to nearly eighty per year. This work plus many orders for canal narrow boats helped keep the skilled workforce together.

Records of craft built before the beginning of the twentieth century are fragmentary. Since that time the building rates at Northwich were as follows:-

	Yarwood	Pimblott	Total per year	Average per year
1900-10	127	119	246	22
1911-20	129	210	339	34
1921-30	192 *	168	360	36
1931-40	292 *	68	360	36
1941-50	203	84	287	29
1951-60	65	83	148	15
1961-71	25	33	58	5
	1033	765	1798	25

* including a large numbers of narrow boats

The decline in the number of vessels constructed in the final two decades largely reflects the increasing complexity of the vessels built.

Initially, the craft were built for local use. In the 1850s over half the 217 Northwich-owned craft had been built in the town. During the twentieth century Northwich-built vessels have served their owners in:-

Aden	Argentina	Australia	Barbados
Brazil	Caribbean	Ceylon	Chile
Christmas Islands	Congo	East Africa	Falklands
Gibraltar	Goa	Greece	Guiana
Holland	Hong Kong	India	Ireland
Italy	Malta	Mauritius	Norway
Portugal	South Africa	Sudan	West Africa

Northwich-built vessels are still serving in about 20 countries. Incidentally Crichton vessels, built at Chester, were also exported to many of the countries listed above.

The British Government ordered many craft from Yarwood and Pimblott. These were for such diverse bodies as, HM Customs & Excise and the White Fish Authority. The yards delivered to the armed services a considerable number of craft. A few of which were commissioned into the Royal Navy and flew the White Ensign. The orders from the services included-

    182 Admiralty (including harbour craft)
    26 War Office
    69 Air Ministry and Ministry of Aircraft Production
    11 Ministry of War Transport

    288

Amongst the craft built for the armed forces were a number of dumb lighters for the carriage of aviation fuel which were ordered by the Admiralty during the Second World War. Of these craft one, the **C643**, was lost on the way to the atomic tests at Christmas Islands. She was replaced by another Yarwood built vessel, the **C600**, which was abandoned at the Pacific island on completion of the tests. Of a different class, the **C609**, a steam-propelled oil-fired vessel, when withdrawn from service had her Yarwood-built engine transferred to a Norwegian veteran steamer the **STORD 1**. The **C626** became a training ship at Plymouth inheriting the famous naval name, **AJAX**.

The Pimblott-built coaster **EMPIRE GROVE,** owned by the Ministry of War Transport, had a notably short career for she was completed on 9 October 1941 and was wrecked near Hartland Point nine days later. Two Northwich-built sisterships of this vessel were at Normandy, one of which is still in service, namely the Pimblott-built **EMPIRE CRICKETER**. This vessel was lengthened in 1971 but in late 1998 she suffered a serious fire which appeared to spell the end for her. However, against all the odds, it was decided to repair her and she continues to work in Denmark under the name **TINY SWAN**.

*With her aft section rebuilt, the **TINY SWAN** arrives at the Danish port of Horsens on 15 October 1999 following her re-entry into service.*
(Bent Mikkelsen)

During the Second World War, the Admiralty ordered two standard classes of self-propelled lighters for the storing of warships. These were the VIC (Victualling Inshore Craft) classes and a total of 98 were built, 25 by Pimblott. The Clyde "puffer" *LASCAR* was the prototype for the first group of 14, all 66 feet long, which were built on the Weaver whilst the second group, of 11, with all welded chine hulls, were 88 feet in length. All Weaver-built VICs were steam powered and coal fired but a few built elsewhere were motor vessels. An order with Pimblott for a further four of the second group was cancelled and the ships involved appear to have been completed for the Anglo Saxon Petroleum Co. Three of these were listed as being still in service in Indonesia in 1998.

Some of the Pimblott-built craft had notable careers. The **VIC 27** became a youth training ship and in the early 1990s was used by the BBC as the **VITAL SPARK** in the remaking of the "Para Handy Tales". **VIC 51** was for a period in 1945 manned by the Royal Netherlands Navy. The **VIC 62** became a calcified seaweed dredger after being used as a trials ship for a new steering system being designed for very large oil tankers. The **VIC 62** was thus used as a large scale model of a supertanker.

*In light grey livery and with her name on the front of the bridge, the **VIC 50** is making cautious progress. The setting is the Hunts Lock bypass channel and she is probably returning to Pimblott's yard from a period in the Weaver Navigation dry dock which was a little further down that arm.*

(J D Smales, Roy Cressey collection)

When the Admiralty decided to replace the numerous tenders, including the VIC craft, in the 1960s, they placed the order for the first six of the new class with Pimblott. Made up of twelve prefabricated sections the craft were 75 feet long and the height of the superstructure was restricted to 23 feet to allow operations under the angled flight deck of aircraft carriers. Each vessel could carry 25 tons of stores or up to 200 standing passengers. Six further tenders were ordered later.

Three of the vessels served overseas. At Gibraltar the **ALNESS** and **ASHCOTT** were pressed into service, despite a top speed of only 10.5 knots, as imitation torpedo boats for the training of passing warships. The **CAWSAND** served at Port Stanley after the Falklands War of 1982. Whilst building the tenders Pimblott also received orders from the Admiralty for four tugs. Two were shipped out to Singapore, for use at the naval base. With the closure of the base the **CELIA** was sold locally. The **CLARE**, however, had already been transferred to Hong Kong. Here she was commissioned and was naval crewed to be employed on anti smuggling and illegal immigrant patrols in the Pearl River estuary. In 1980 she strayed into Chinese waters and negotiations had to be initiated for her return. Whilst used in this role the tug was fitted with a Gemini dinghy and could mount light machine guns. She returned to normal duties in 1981 and was placed on the disposal list in 1985.

FRODSHAM

The history of Frodsham as a port dates back to at least the reign of Edward I. The earliest recorded ship built there was a 40 ton sloop named **ARMITAGE**, in 1728. Of the 60 vessels recorded as Frodsham built, only two exceeded 100 tons. Shipbuilding ended in 1862. Output of the Frodsham yards was not considerable, with an average of one launch every twenty-seven months. However as 3 ships were built in 1793, 4 in 1802, 3 in 1839 and 4 in 1858, it can be seen that there would be long periods when no building was being undertaken. As if to demonstrate this point, although the last ship was built in 1862, it was not until 1866 that the yard and its contents were put up for sale. The yard was located just to the north of the railway viaduct, on the east bank.

Due to the small size and workaday nature of the craft built, little information on the vessels remains. One vessel, the flat **ANN**, built in 1799, has earned a place in history, as her loss on 18 October 1858 while passing through Bardsey Sound has been recorded in a Welsh sea shanty. Despite their size, not all Frodsham built craft were confined to the Mersey or coastal voyages. Another **ANN**, 35 tons and built in 1737, is known to have voyaged to the West Indies on at least one occasion.

The **JANE & ANN**, of Carnarvon (sic), 57 registered tons, was a two-masted schooner built at Frodsham in 1816 and she survived until 1920. She ran aground in the River Ribble and could not be salved. She was subsequently sold for breaking up.

*A one-time flat, now being used as a clubhouse, rests on the site of the former shipyard at Frodsham. The vessel is possibly the **STANTONDALE**, built about 1926 by Yarwood as the **NIGEL VERNON**.*
(Author)

WINSFORD

Building of flats at Winsford commenced not long after the Weaver was made navigable. By the time of the formation of the Salt Union Company in 1888, which took over the majority of salt producers, there were six properly equipped shipyards. These were owned by Cross, Deakin, Evans, Falk, Stubbs and Verdin. Following the merger, work became concentrated on the former Deakin yard, which had launched three flats in six weeks in 1861. This yard also produced the last and largest Winsford-built ship. The **MONARCH** was launched on 6 August 1896, of which more later. Although the other yards had closed, this yard continued to repair Salt Union and later ICI craft until the 1950s.

The most innovative vessels built at Winsford were the four craft built in the 1860s by Herman Falk, who was also the owner of the Meadowbank Salt Mine, as well as a shipbuilder. The series commenced with the iron hulled steamer **EXPERIMENT**, followed by the modified **DEVELOPMENT**, and then the **IMPROVEMENT** and lastly the **SUPPLEMENT**. The introduction of these, the first steam ships built for the salt trade, revolutionised the movement of salt on the Weaver. Not only could they make more voyages per year, they could tow up to three sailing flats at the same time. They were quickly followed by many more steam craft.

Other notable craft from Winsford included the **ALBION** and the **DOLPHIN** which were requisitioned to support the Home Fleet at Scapa Flow during the First World War. The **NIL DESPERANDUM** was built by George Deakin in 1867 and lasted 81 years. During this time she served in the Deakin, Salt Union and ICI fleets. Even after a sinking due to colliding with a submerged wreck during the Second World War she was deemed worth returning to service. The end came in 1948, but even then not without drama. Stripped of any useful fittings the hulk was taken to Winsford Flash to be scuttled. However, the old craft would not sink until explosives had been used to blow a hole in her stern.

Mention has already been made of the **MONARCH**, the last ship built at Winsford. Following her launch she was found to be too large to pass under the old low-level stone bridge at Hartford, now replaced by a high-level bridge carrying the Northwich Bypass over the river. To get round this obstacle all fittings had to be removed from the deck of the vessel, a cargo of salt as ballast was added and divers had to dredge a channel under the bridge. Not surprisingly she did not return to her birth place. Her end came whilst being used as a collier when she was wrecked of the Irish coast during the First World War.

*This postcard, available in the Salt Museum, shows the launch of the **MONARCH** in 1896.*

(Cheshire Museum Service)

TYPES OF CRAFT BUILT IN CHESHIRE

Barges	Wide and narrow types for canals, both powered and dumb, plus larger craft for loading and unloading larger ships in harbour.
Beacons & Buoys	Floating navigation marks
Bombscows	Powered barges for carrying bombs to larger ships or flying boats
Canoes	55 foot long canoes for use on West African beaches
Cargo ships	Including the Weaver vessels sometimes called "packets" and general coasters
Canal cruisers	Pleasure craft
Dredgers	Both grab and suction type.
Ferries	Passenger craft
Fishing boats	Small number only built
Flats	The traditional sail or man/horse drawn Weaver cargo barge; larger versions sailed to ports from Anglesey to the Solway
Grain Elevator	Suction vessel for extracting grain from ships holds to silos
Launches	Used for all sorts of communications around harbours in the UK and in harbours and rivers in Africa and elsewhere
Pontoons	Small landing stages, or craft for mooring next to vessels undergoing repair
Puffers	Small cargo craft used on the West Coast of Scotland
Punts	Small flat bottomed work craft; also clinker-built work boats carried by all small commercial vessels.
Surf boats	Used in India and West Africa to unload cargo where harbours had yet to be built. Usually had crew of 8 oarsmen plus a coxswain
Tankers	Used for the carriage of liquid cargoes.
Tenders	Communications craft, mainly for the Admiralty
Tugs	For use on canals, rivers and in harbours

The **LA MAUVE** (Jersey Norman French for "seagull") was built by J Crichton & Co Ltd at Saltney as yard number 544. An unpowered buoy tender, she was completed in September 1935 for the States of Jersey (Harbours and Airport Committee). On completion, she was towed to Jersey by the steam coaster **HOVE** which was bringing a cargo to the island at the time. *LA MAUVE* remained in service until the early 1970s and was then laid up in St Aubins harbour for many years before being finally scuttled off Bouley Bay on Jersey's north-east coast about 1989.

(Dave Hocquard)

NORTHWICH SHIPS - PHOTO FEATURE

The **ALNESS**, an Admiralty tender, was built by Pimblott and launched on 18 June 1964. It was this vessel, along with the Pimblott-built **ASHCOTT**, which served as an imitation torpedo boat at Gibraltar where she was offered for disposal in 1986. Other ships of the class included the **ALNMOUTH** and **APPLEBY** which were used by the Sea Cadet Corps until 1998. The **APPLEBY** was transferred to the fledgling Marine Volunteer Service which replaced the former Royal Naval Auxiliary Service; a similar fate may await the **ALNMOUTH**. If so, these two vessels should be seen around the coast of the UK for several years to come.

(Dave Hocquard)

The Pimblott built **LOYAL GOVERNOR** was one of four 75-foot long tenders. She was commissioned into the Royal Navy and renamed **ALERT,** in 1976, to take part in "Operation Interknit". This involved the carrying out of inshore patrols and surveillance tasks off the coast of Northern Ireland, to stop IRA gun running and other activities.

The photograph was taken at Glasson Dock in 1999 after an extra deckhouse had been added.

(Author)

Yarwood built 13 tugs for the Admiralty, whilst Pimblott built four. The **CHRISTINE**, a sister ship of the **CLARE** (see page 26) was built by Pimblott. The **CHRISTINE** spent all of her life at Devonport, until sold to Scottish owners in 1990. In the photograph she is seen along side a "T" class nuclear submarine.

(Author)

Mention has already been made of the naval service of the **LOYAL GOVERNOR** and the **CLARE**. Three true warships were also built on the Weaver. Yarwood built the Seaward Defence Boat **MARLINGFORD**, whilst Pimblott built two sisters, **DROXFORD** and **MONTFORD**. Part of a class of 20 vessels designed to hunt submarines, in harbour approaches. Many went straight into reserve or were transferred to Commonwealth navies. Armed with one 40mm gun, two depth charge throwers and two depth charge racks. The craft were capable of 18 knots.

The photograph shows the launch of **MONTFORD** at the Pimblott yard on 10 October 1957. After a period in the Reserve Fleet, **MONTFORD** was transferred to the Royal Nigerian Navy and renamed **IBADAN**. Taken over by the Biafran rebel independence forces in May 1967, she was renamed **VIGILANT** but was sunk in action at Port Harcourt on 10 September that year.

DROXFORD spent many years on training duties before being converted into a target vessel. In this role she was initially based at Milford Haven but later in Scotland. In 1999, the suggestion was made that she should be returned to Northwich for restoration as a monument to the shipbuilding industry of the town. **MARLINGFORD**, after a period in the Reserve Fleet, served in the Far East, before disposal in 1967.   (Cheshire Record Office)

As well as the **SAND SWALLOW II** (see pages 20/21) about 100 craft were built for Lever Brothers and their subsidiaries, including Crossfield of Warrington and the United Africa Company. Levers sold their fleet in the late 1970s and early 1980s. The **LUX**, which had been renamed **SAFEHAND**, was sold to a Merseyside owner who operates her in the Liverpool dock system, where she was photographed in original guise on 21 October 1974. The **RINSO** was bought by Irish owners for whom she worked as **FINN VALLEY OIL** until scuttled off Killybegs, County Donegal, in 1997.
                    (Neil Burns)

The 1961 Yarwood-built tug **NORTHWICH** was designed for river work and could operate as a pusher tug, hence the pronounced pushing knee at the bow. She remained in service on the river for 32 years. She is pictured at Frodsham following her sale in 1993.

(Author)

Again built by Yarwood, in 1946, the iron tug **BEESTON** was ordered by the LMS Railway Company. Prior to nationalisation, a number of railway companies operated canal fleets, sometimes to stifle competition and sometimes to supplement their own services. The **BEESTON**, which could also serve as an ice breaker, is shown awaiting restoration at the Ellesmere Port Boat Museum in 1996.

(Author)

The **CERES** was built in 1961 by Pimblott for towing grain barges in Liverpool docks and the Manchester Ship Canal. She remained in service for twenty years before passing to an owner in Ayr. In 1983 she was "swopped" for the similar tug owned by Lagan Marine Services, of Northern Ireland, but seven years later the tugs returned to their respective owners. The **CERES** is still based at Ayr.

(Author)

MSC DIANA was one of eight similar tugs built for the Manchester Ship Canal Company by Pimblott between 1953 and 1960. Designed to support the dredging activities, they followed three earlier and smaller tugs built in 1950. When the Ship Canal Company contracted out its towing operations, six of the tugs were sold. Of the original eight, **MSC DAWN** and **MSC DAINTY** were retained. The **MSC DARING** and **MSC DAPHNE** eventually ended up in West Africa. The remaining four, **MSC DOLPHIN**, (since broken up) **MSC DEBORAH**, **MSC DIDO** and **MSC DIANA** were sold for service on the Thames, where the **DIANA** was photographed near Tower Bridge in 1995.

Of the three earlier tugs only the **MSC APPLETON** remains, having been retained for use on the Ship Canal.

(Author)

The Alexandra Towing Company, became a major customer of the Yarwood yard, with ten tugs being ordered between 1957 and 1964. The group included the Alexandra Towing Company's first motor tug. Eight of the group were similar to the **BROCKLEBANK.** All were engaged in general towage duties at Southampton, the South Wales ports, Liverpool and later Felixstowe. Over the ensuing years they have been sold out of the fleet for further use in Italy, Greece and the Caribbean.

The **BROCKLEBANK** is normally to be found berthed at the Merseyside Maritime Museum at Albert Dock, Liverpool along with the Northwich-built **WINCHAM**.

(Author)

The **MALEMBA** was a twin-screw motor vessel built for the United Africa Company to be used at Calabar, Nigeria. She measured 92 feet by 23 feet with a draught of almost 7 feet. After trials, the vessel was split into two sections which were each towed to Liverpool for shipment and re-assembly at the destination. The two 40-foot derricks each had a lift of 2 tons. Fitted with two galleys, one for Europeans and the other for local crew members, the European accommodation also had at least one shower but there is no mention of such a facility for the rest of the crew. She was built by Yarwood in 1950 and was still in service 25 years later.

(Cheshire Record Office)

Another major towing company to order tugs was the Rea Towing Group which ordered 7 tugs between 1958 and 1964. All but one of the vessels came from the Yarwood yard. The **BEECHGARTH** was designed for use at Liverpool, a role she fulfilled for 32 years before being sold to a Cornish Company and renamed **MOUNTS BAY**. She is now in private ownership and is named **GYM** under the Honduran flag.

The two tugs astern of the **BEECHGARTH** are the **KILGARTH** and the **FOYLEGARTH**. Both were built by Yarwood in 1958 as the **KILMORE** and **FOYLEMORE** for the Johnston Warren Line, to serve at Liverpool. Purchased by the Rea Group in 1969 the **FOYLEGARTH** now serves as the **ST BUDO**C at Falmouth whilst her sister has found her way out to Greece.

NOTE The small coaster in the far distance is ICI's **MARBURY**, built by Pimblott 1949 and still listed in Lloyd's Register as the Honduran-flagged **SAN JUAN**,   (Author)

SEIONT II, built 1935 by Yarwood, was used both as a dredger and as a buoy tender at Caernarfon. The 87 foot long vessel spent the whole of her life working in the Menai area, until withdrawn in 1979. Following withdrawal she was purchased by the National Museum of Wales who allocated management to the Seiont II Maritime Trust, based at Victoria Dock, Caernarfon.

Between 1984 and 1986 the vessel was extensively refurbished on the Mersey. It was claimed that the work then carried out should enable the craft to last for at least a further 50 years. Despite these claims she was sadly broken up in 1999 although it was felt by many that a worthwhile preservation effort could be launched. These two photographs show her at Port Dinorwic awaiting demolition (left) and with demolition underway (below).   (Author)

The **FRANCES POOLE** was built by Yarwood in 1926 and served all her life on the Weaver and the Mersey. In the main she delivered ICI export cargoes to Liverpool Docks from the Winnington and Wallerscote installations. It was such a voyage that found her berthed at North Huskisson Dock on the night of 3/4 May 1941. On this night the steamer **MALAKAND,** loaded with 1000 tons of explosives, caught fire and exploded during a bombing raid. The dock, the **MALAKAND** and several other craft were destroyed.

The **FRANCES POOLE** was later sold to the Liverpool Lighterage Company eventually being broken up at Runcorn in 1977. The photograph shows particularly well the layout of a typical Weaver Packet.

(ICI Mond Division)

The **AESTUS** was a twin-screw tender built for the Mersey Docks & Harbour Board by Yarwood in 1945. Used for various tasks including surveying, she remained in the Board's service for 32 years. Sold in 1981 to a Liverpool firm who planned to use her for contract work, this role continued until the **AESTUS** was broken up at Birkenhead in February 1986. The photograph shows her lifted out of the water at Liverpool in the mid-1970s.

(Author)

Many canal craft were built on the Weaver. Barges can be broadly divided into narrowboats and wide boats. The latter were built for those canals where the locks are 14 feet wide instead of the more normal 7 feet.

The **BACUP**, built by Yarwood in 1950, was a wide craft, delivered for use on the Leeds Liverpool Canal. Because the locks on part of this canal were shorter than usual, the **BACUP** had the distinction of being a wide short boat, being 62 feet long by 14 feet wide with a cargo capacity of 50 tons. Withdrawn in 1982 she passed to the Ellesmere Port Boat Museum for preservation.

(Author)

The largest dredger built by Yarwood, the **GOOLE BIGHT**, was constructed in 1957 to serve the dock system at Goole in Yorkshire. The picture shows her working there 39 years later in the colours of her privatised owners Associated British Ports. Early in 2000, she was sold to owners in Hartlepool where she found a new lease of life undertaking dredging operations connected with a new marina. Indeed she is probably working harder now than at any previous stage of her life.

(Author)

To help keep the yard going in the depressed 1930s, Yarwood built over 200 canal narrow boats , two of which were the **REGULUS** and **RADIANT**. Built for the Grand Union Canal Carrying Company, this pair of narrow boats was launched on 14 November 1935 and were part of what became known as the "Middle Northwich Class".

The **RADIANT** served as a pump barge during the Second World War and then as a maintenance/hopper barge on the River Avon. The **REGULUS**, the unpowered butty barge, was also used as a hopper barge, before being left derelict. Both were purchased, in 1993, and reunited. Restoration has been undertaken by the new owners and the craft can often be seen on north west canals.

(Author)

The Weaver was the birth place of many commercial vessels, but few pleasure craft. Pimblott built some cabin cruisers, in later years, but Yarwood built a remarkable vessel in 1927. The **LA GOLETA** was the only racing yacht built on the river. Owned by Ralph Peverley, of Ellesmere Port and designed by W S Tallman of Pittsburgh USA she weighed 30 tons was 54 feet long, overall, and had a beam of 12 feet 9 inches. The hull was made of English oak with pitch pine planking and iron fastenings.

She was designed to take part in the 1927, 615 mile, Fastnet Race. This she did with distinction, being the first round the Fastnet Rock and the first across the finishing line. She was however placed second, on handicap. To come second in the race was a no mean feat, particularly as only two craft finished, out of 15 starters! After the race she was sold to owners in the Isle of Wight and passed through various others owners over the ensuing years. In 1959, after a period of idleness, she was re rigged and used as a sail training ship along the West Coast of Scotland. A further major rebuild took place in the late 1960s. She is believed to be still in existence.   (Author, courtesy of Mid-Cheshire College)

Yarwood built one narrow boat for the Samuel Barlow Coal Company of Glascote, near Tamworth and that was in 1938. Yarwood only built the hull, the cabin and other fittings being installed elsewhere. After many years trading the **BEATTY** was converted to pleasure use, this was the fate of many former working boats. Pictured here at Chester, in 1995, her traditional lines have not been lost.

(Author)

Shell's refinery complex at Stanlow straddles the Manchester Ship Canal. In order to ferry workers across the Canal, Yarwood built two ferries in 1965. Named **MSC CONVEYOR** and **MSC CARRIER**, the latter was photographed on 30 August 1997. Each vessel is 28 feet 6 inches long and is permitted to carry 12 passengers in addition to a crew of 1 and 15 cwt of cargo.
(Author)

Another vessel built for the Manchester Ship Canal Company but this time by Pimblott in 1951. The photograph shows the 21-ton **MSC BENNETT** being lifted out of the water at the Canal Company's Old Quay Yard, Runcorn, on 15 October 1987. The purpose of the lift was to facilitate her being broken up for spares.
(Colin Leonard)

The **BARMERE** was one of a large group of barges built by Yarwood and Pimblott for the Manchester Ship Canal Company between 1948 and 1957. Measuring 71 feet by 14 feet 6 inches, she was used to carry grain to the Kellogg's factory in Manchester. Once her trading days were over, the next stage in her career saw her used for rubbish collection in the Liverpool dock system before she was sold on to the Sankey Canal Restoration Society. In 1989 she was taken by road to a site in St Helens ready to be restored for use as an exhibition venue on the now land-locked canal. This photograph, taken ten years later, shows that the ambition has yet to be realised.
(Author)

(Left) The **FREDERICK WHITTINGHAM** is a tender built by Yarwood in 1934 for the City of London by whom she was used on the River Thames. Sold in the late 1970s, she is seen here at a boat rally in Northwich soon after her sale.

(Ron Townson)

The barge **ASH** was built by Yarwood in 1935 for the Erewash Canal Company. With the ending of commercial carrying on the narrow canals, the **ASH**, like many other barges, became a pleasure craft. Retaining her original profile, she is now used as a camping barge. In the 1970s she was paired with the Yarwood-built **YEOFORD** but in this photograph, taken at Chester in 1998, she is paired with the Pimblott-built Admiral class barge **COLLINGWOOD**. Three years earlier, the **COLLINGWOOD** had been used as a support vessel on the Birmingham to London walk organised by the St John Ambulance Brigade.

(Author)

The **RN AIR 2A** was one of a group of lighters designed by Yarwood but only this and **RN AIR 3A** were built by the company. Self-propelled, these 131-foot long vessels could ferry aircraft from the dockside to the aircraft carrier or other ship on which they were to be used. The fate of **RN AIR 2A** is not clear, but **RN AIR 3A** was sold and converted to a ferry in Norway. Reports about the fate of this vessel differ - some say that she was scuttled in 1991 but others affirm that she still existed in 1998. The photograph is of a model in the library of the Mid-Cheshire College, Hartford, and is reproduced by kind permission of the college. (Author)

The dredger **RAMSGATE** was built in 1962 for work at the port from which she takes her name, replacing an earlier vessel of the same name. Her duties include the dredging of the harbour entrance and berths. As the dredger is crewed on a day basis, there are no overnight berths provided for the crew.

This sequence of photographs shows her at various stages during construction at the Yarwood yard. The bow view (above) shows clearly the numbered frames. It also offers an insight into construction methods. The equipment in the foreground is of special note. The stern view (below) seems to have been taken on the same day.

The three photographs on this page were taken on the day of the launch. Much of the equipment seen in the photograph on the previous page has now been utilised to assist in the launching operation.

The **RAMSGATE** touches water for the first time.

Much fitting out work still remains. Dredging gear, bridge equipment and controls, anchors and deck fittings clearly need to be added.

(All photographs courtesy of the East Kent Maritime Trust.)

There is little doubt that the Northwich yards became synonymous with vessels built for ICI and its predecessors. On this page we look at just three examples, all built by Yarwood.

In the photographs above and left, we see the **JAMES JACKSON GRUNDY**, built in 1948. She was sold to the Northwich Sea Cadets for £1 and renamed **TS WITCH**. For many years she has been berthed at the site of the former Yarwood yard.

The **WINCHAM** was one of nine new vessels built for ICI between 1944 and 1949. Three were steam powered, the others had diesel engines. All were 102 feet long and 23 feet beam; they could carry some 300 tons of cargo. The 1948-built **WINCHAM**, seen here transhipping a bulk cargo to the **PORT INVERCARGILL**, was sold to Bulk Cargo Handling Services, of Liverpool. When she was surplus to their needs, she was sold for preservation. Normally she is moored opposite the Merseyside Maritime Museum. A sister vessel, the **COMBERBACH**, can be found at the Boat Museum, Ellesmere Port.

*The **CRESCENT** was built for Brunner Mond in 1910. She was sold to Richard Abel and Company in 1963 and was renamed **CALESDALE**, only to be broken up four years later*

*Another vessel built for Brunner Mond, the **MADGE** dates from 1912. After fifty years service, she was sold to the Liverpool Lighterage Company which used her on the River Mersey for a few more years. She is seen heading downriver from the ICI Wallerscote works in a photograph thought to date from April 1958.*

(All photographs on this and the previous page are reproduced with kind permission from the ICI Mond Division)

INDEX OF SHIPS

INDEX OF BUILDERS AND YARDS

BIBLIOGRAPHY

In addition to the named donors of photographs, to whom grateful thanks are offered, the following sources have been used and their help is gratefully acknowledged.

Primary sources :
Cheshire and Chester Record Office; Ellesmere Port Boat Museum; Flintshire Record Office; Grosvenor Museum; Merseyside Maritime Museum; The Salt Museum; Warrington Museum, Yarwoods Yark Book.

Periodicals :
Coastal Shipping; Marine News (Journal of the World Ship Society)*; Sea Breezes; Ships Monthly; Waterways World.*

Books :
Lloyd's Register of Shipping; Barlows (Alan Faulkner, Rothwell, 1986); *Mersey Rovers* (Roy Fenton, Kendal, 1997); *W J Yarwood & Sons Ltd* (Clive Guthrie, Northwich); *Fifty Years of Naval Tugs* (B Hannan, Liskeard); *Chester and the River Dee* (ed A M Kennett, Chester, 1982);*Mersey and Weaver Flats* (E Paget Tomlinson, Kettering, 1973); *The Rise and Fall of Parkgate* (G Place, Manchester, 1994); *Mersey Flats and Flatmen* (Michael Stammers, Liverpool, 1993); *Schooner Port* (H F Starkey, Ormskirk, 1983); *Too Many Boats* (R Wilson, Kettering, 1980).

The author wishes to place on record his grateful thanks to Gil Mayes who has checked the manuscript with great care, and has added important details to the histories of some of the vessels listed. Any errors remain the responsibility of the author who apologises in advance for such errors which remain.

Every effort has been made to establish the copyright of all photographs used.

WARRINGTON BANK-QUAY FOUNDRY.

To be LET, with immediate possession, for a term of years, if required, that large and convenient SHIP-BUILDING and BOILER YARD, together with spacious FOUNDRIES, SMITHIES, GUNMILL, SHEDS, &c., known as the "BANK-QUAY FOUNDRY," Warrington.

The Premises extend from the London and Northwestern Railway (with which there is communication by siding) to the River Mersey, and are furnished with Engine-power, Wharf-crane, and every convenience for carrying on an extensive business in Ship-building and Engineering.

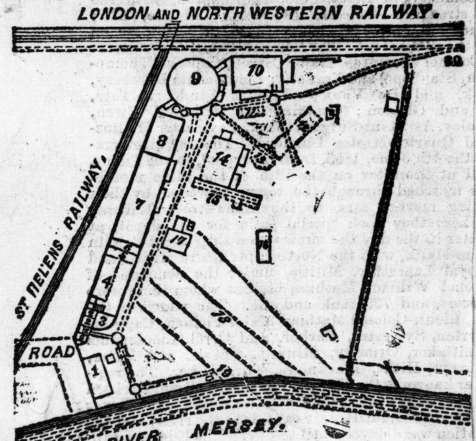

REFERENCE TO PLAN.

1—Stores, 22 yards by 10 ; 2—Offices ; 3—Drawing-office, with Pattern-shops over ; 4—Joiners' Shop and Shed, 30 yards by 15, with Model-rooms over ; 5—Sawpits ; 6—Stables ; 7—Smithy and Machine Shop, 54 yards by 15 ; 8—Foundry ; 9—Foundry, 28 yards diameter ; 10—Gun Mill ; 11—Gun Chipping Shed ; 12—Travelling Crane ; 13—Shear Legs and Top ; 14—Platers' Shed and Keel Smithy ; 15—Circular Saw Mill ; 16—Plate Shed, 17—Platers' Furnace and Shed ; 18—Ships' Ways ; 19—Wharf Crane ; 20—Railway Siding.

Apply to Mr. EDWARD TAYLEUR, Vulcan Foundry, near Warrington ; or to Mr. SAMUEL HOLME, Benson-street, Liverpool.

The sale notice of Bank Quay Yard. This illustration must date from the late 1850's, (see page15).

Sketch map showing location of shipyards mentioned in the text (not to scale)

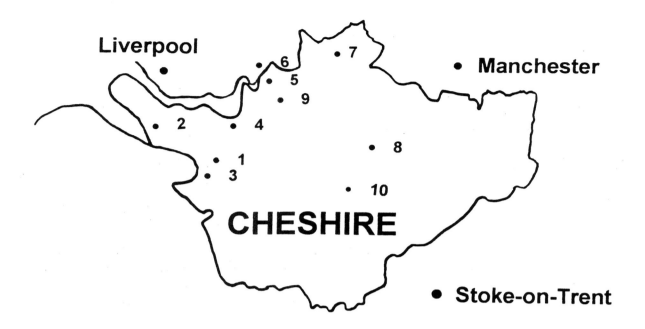

Key to locations:

1. Chester

2. Parkgate and Neston

3. Saltney

4. Ellesmere Port

5. Runcorn

6. Widnes

7. Warrington (including Sankey Bridges)

8. Northwich

9. Frodsham

10. Winsford